Life Through The Storm
The Journey of Forgiveness
by Stormie G. Steele, Ph.D

I0212895

Published by Stormie G. Steele, Ph.D at Smashwords

Copyright 2015

Life Through The Storm
The Journey of Forgiveness
A 21 Day Journey of Insightful Principles
Stormie G. Steele, Ph.D

Cover Design by Cover Creator

Cover Images by Pamela's Fresh Look Photography

Design Concept by Stormie

Smashwords Edition, License Notes

This ebook is licensed for your personal enjoyment only. This ebook may not be re-sold or given away to other people. If you would like to share this book with another person, please purchase an additional copy for each recipient. If you're reading this book and did not purchase it, or it was not purchased for your use only, then please return to Smashwords.com and purchase your own copy. Thank you for respecting the hard work of this author.

This book is dedicated to my children, and all others whom I've ever offended

Jmalo, Rachel, Rebekah & Robin ~
I am honored to have held you in my arms, to have nurtured you - to have kissed & loved
you... to experience you loving me.

Know that my limited knowledge of parenthood is fully expressed through love.

Forgive me, I am sorry to have caused any offense against you...

Acknowledgments

To my husband, my children & grandchildren~
You each remind me of what it means to be loved unconditionally.

Thank you for bringing life, laughter and value to our relationship. ~Storm

First, I am grateful to God my Father for teaching me that life holds numerous hidden treasures, often hidden within the challenges of pain and disappointment. It is through those encounters that I've learned to call and rely upon the greatest Source of my life. Thank you Father for your enduring love, grace and mercy on my behalf...I am internally and eternally grateful that You've allowed me to become more than my experiences.

My husband, the love of my life, companion & counselor-friend, Rev. Dr. J.V. Steele. You are my Divine hook-up! Love, I really appreciate your presence in my life, world and affairs Thank you for your time, commitment and dedication on my behalf. Your supportive partnership is phenomenal - your keen eye for editing and the smooth flow that it has created for this project is evident. Your faith in me pushes me towards unimaginable heights! Thank you for your counsel, insights & constructive advice JV...I thank our Lord for you!

To my children (maternal) - Jmalo, Rachel (Jimmie), Rebekah & Robin (Aaron) – Jessica & Katina (inherited). The things that many of us seek - love, acceptance, validation, and purpose becomes realized when we're in intimate union with our God & His Son, Jesus. We are flawed humans, there are no perfect experiences, we are left with the authority to create healthy and loving encounters. We hurt, we cry, we learn, we grow...we forgive – we heal! Your life is not contingent on what "they" did or didn't do, it's ultimately about you taking ownership! Our wholeness exists in our Creator God - Who has ALL to do with us!

To my loving & intelligent grandchildren (maternally & inherited) – Aaron, Amyri, Arielle, Ashton Noah, Ashton, Ayanna, Ebony, Hannah, Israel, Jewell, Joshua, Kyia, Kailyn, Kaley, Kiera, Langston & Olivia - you each possess a unique expression of identity, strength, character & courage. Never compromise who you are, nor your convictions! Always seek to know your Creator God - align yourself with His principals and His ways. Nothing or no one else can ever fill what He alone can fill!

Dad, I love you – it's a complete joy communing with you. Thank you for your prayers, and for being the presence that you are in my life!

To my **sisters & brothers** – Camille, Charles, Deborah (whom I call twin) I am thankful and humbled by your seeds of faith and timely investment! Jeanae', Kenneth, Lorenzo, Pam – Thank you for your faith in me, and the beautiful photography (cover images), Sheena, Timothy, Tina, Tony & Tonya - **sisters in love**, Alicia, Benita, Dorothy & Portia (The late Emily Steele-Perry (whose health fair brought Jim & I together) – **brothers in love** – Bill, Maurice & Tal, cousins, nieces, nephews, **aunt & uncle** (Henry & Maxine White), step-family members, friends & a host of others - whose faith, patience, wisdom, prayers & love continue to support me. Thank you all for being a part of my life's journey and for the many, many lessons that I've embraced as a result of your presence in my life! You are invaluable...I love you!

Margeah Bey, the loving mother presence in my life. I love & appreciate you!

Carolyn Joy – your insights into my creativity helped to birth its reality. I treasure your love, your prayers and your sisterhood!

Jud and Rose Phillips (Phillips Entertainment) - I am grateful for your time and energy...your faith in me continues to sprout new seeds. I appreciate you both.

Table of Contents

Preface

Introduction

Using This Book as A Tool

Day 1
Forgiveness ~A Practice of Disciplines

Day 2
Forgiveness ~The Ability To Alter The Moment

Day 3
Forgiveness ~A Blessing!

Day 4
Forgiveness ~A Walk in Mercy, Compassion and Love

Day 5
Forgiveness and Deep Breathing

Day 6
Forgiveness ~ Imperfections, Growth & Development

Day 7
Forgiveness ~No Personal Attacks

Day 8
Forgiveness and Self-acceptance

Day 9
Forgiveness Virtues

Day 10
Forgiveness ~Seize The Evolution!

Day 11
Forgiveness ~The Offender

Day 12
The Alteration of Forgiveness

Day 13
Forgiveness ~Know That You Are Loved

Day 14
Forgiveness ~Not an Easy Task

Day 15
Forgiveness ~The Command of Quiet

Day 16
Forgiveness ~Waking up from A Bad Dream,

Day 17
Imagine Forgiveness

Day 18
Resentment, an Inner Alarm

Day 19
Lessons in Forgiveness

Day 20
Forgiveness ~Seventy Times Seventy

Day 21
Forgiveness ~Reconciliation

A Brief Prayer for Your Journey of Forgiveness

About The Author

Preface

We all have had moments when we were hurt or offended by someone – moments when we've hurt, or offended someone. Whether the offense was committed intentionally or unintentionally is not the concern of the offended, rather - the concern is that of having been offended.

Unforgiveness is the prerequisite of bitterness and resentment. It is the dark fruit that invades the inner-lives of its possessors, controlling their lives with interruptions of unedited replays of pain. It can become a cycle of madness, a ritual of self-injury - a rhythm that distorts the whole of who we are...love.

We have all been hurt on one level or another. Some of us are inclined to let it go, while others carry the burden of unforgiveness for the rest of their lives. Those who are burdened are usually filled with stories of hurt, blame and resentment without relief. Relief often does not explain why we were hurt, rather, it releases us from the discomfort of anger, and from the agony of defining ourselves through pain.

Forgiveness is a matter of self preservation, a matter of personal dignity and a resolution for healing. Forgiveness does not condone the offense, it releases its victims from the potential of long-term dis-ease.

If someone offends you without acknowledging the offense, usually done with an apology or other, move on. We can't control the behavior of others, nor the WHYS to their seeming lack of compassion – but we do control our own behavior! While we ponder the matter of forgiving others, it is crucial that we become fully aware that we too have offended – intentionally and unintentionally – least we forget that we also have caused pain.

Forgiveness is resulted through the process of time, patience, self-examination, honesty and many other factors that come to aid our healing. Healing and forgiveness are synonymous, it's rare to hold one without the other.

We are capable of forgiving, whether we realize it or not. It is a Divine requirement for wholeness and well-being. Forgiveness deep cleanses our inner-core – teaching and reminding us that we are not to be defined by the impact of experiences that appear to dictate that we are less than capable of being whole.

The Journey of Forgiveness is to remind you of its essential significance, as it relates to many of our present relationships and those that will become a part of our future experiences. Forgiveness has a way of keeping us on course, of reminding us to prioritize our emotions, and our perspectives as we interact with others.

Forgiveness is a worthy and humbling virtue. It instructs us to live mindful and compassionate towards our fellow travelers – as we too have the capacity to offend.

I am not oblivious or immune to offenses – I merely seek to be whole.
~Storm

Life Through The Storm: The Journey of Forgiveness

INTRODUCTION

My life has been a series of events - fortunate and unfortunate, expected and unexpected, welcomed and unwelcome...familiar and unfamiliar - each with its unique seed of purpose, designed to bring forth life.

Life has a way of escorting us through various experiences that seem to dictate the outcome of who we are to become, and of who we are not. We are not bound to live by our experiences alone; however, they do play a significant part in the developmental process of our makeup. Our experiences are lessons - all of them, filled with power and possibility...either to destroy, or to bring forth life!

It behooves us to know what we believe, to honor our convictions, to be mindful of our emotions, our thoughts and our behavior as we interact with life. As all share part in the sacredness of our journey.

I do not believe that life has singled out anyone of us for harsh encounters - we are born into sin. The result of being born into sin does not alleviate the truth of God's love, nor His plan for our lives. Life's rhythm is that of joy, pain and gain, laughter, birth and death...and the flow of constant change.

"For I know the plans that I have for you, declares the LORD, plans for welfare and not evil, to give you a future and a hope."
~Jeremiah 29:11 (ESV)

Life Through The Storm: The Journey of Forgiveness

INTRODUCTION

One of my most treasured memories is that of being a child. The innocence of knowing love, laughter and fun made an enormous impact upon my soul. I loved being a little girl! My early memories of childhood are quite significant, as it was a time when I began to form some of the most vital aspects of my identity - courage, strength, self-confidence and freedom!

As a child (between the ages of 1 – 6), I possessed a strong sense of knowing what I wanted, or did not want. I was very decisive. I remember no thoughts or feelings of being unloved, nor of being unsure of my sense of self. As a matter of fact, I was quite sure that I liked myself and equally loved myself.

I loved to write, read, color, and draw. Tasting food and the feel of the grass on my bare feet was a delight. The joy of the warm summer wind on my skin opened wonders to my senses as a child.

Those memories carved into my essence the pleasure and enjoyment of simplicity. I am blessed to have recollection of those precious times - they are priceless and continue to add volumes to my present!

As a child I was always aware of a presence that I acknowledged as God and believed that I was being watched over. I imagined that God was attempting to speak to me – attempting to get my attention through the sound of the wind that seemed to whistle everyday. I'd whistle in response to the sound of the wind, as though a secret message was occurring between us. I now define that wind as the Holy Spirit.

"I am with you always, even unto the end of the ages."

(Matthew 28:20 b) NKJV

Life Through The Storm: The Journey of Forgiveness

INTRODUCTION

Many of aforementioned memories would become cloudy, as the next 7 years of my life were altered by abuse. I will not go into the details of the abuse that I experienced, rather I will focus on its impact, and on the process of regaining hope, identity, character, healing...and forgiveness.

"The thief comes only to steal, and kill and destroy. I am come that they may have life, and have it abundantly." (John 10:10) ESV

It's easy to hide from the pain and shame of past experiences - whether caused by others, or ourselves. Hiding does not resolve issues, nor does lingering in unforgiveness - it is not a healthy resolution.

When we suppress things that need to be acknowledged - worked on and worked through - we open for ourselves windows of instability. It need not take years of broken relationships, low self-esteem, hiding behind success, drinking, drugs and a host of other self-destructive habits before the journey of forgiveness begins.

When we are willing to commit to the process of time - and all that it warrants (full participation) - the healing alteration of forgiveness takes place. We alone, and God within us are left with doing the work. Trust me - it is a worthy investment of time and energy.

I believe that forgiveness is a result of attentive cooperation with time, and a commitment to further gain insight of ourselves as we process life. It is essential that we remind ourselves - we can come to know life and meaning despite our past experiences.

My ultimate reason to forgive those who interrupted the innocence of my childhood was out of a determination to live (not merely survive), and to preserve self-dignity, and respect for my life.

"Those who are well have no need of a physician, but those who are sick"
~Luke 5:31 (NKJV)

"Physician heal thyself"
~Luke 4:23 (NKJV)

Life Through The Storm: The Journey of Forgiveness

INTRODUCTION

The Journey of Forgiveness is a response to the voice of inner truths, briefly appearing within anyone of us before it vanishes within the clouds of distraction. I have chosen to capture its brevity as best as possible.

Within the pages of Life through The Storm: The Journey of Forgiveness, my intent is to express in a conversation style that fellow seekers can relate to. I also want to acknowledge the possibility that resides within each one of us. As we connect with our own ability to heal, we also gain a sense of practical immediacy that can be utilized daily.

The Journey of Forgiveness is a personal, and empowering adherence to Divine counsel.

"Counsel in the heart of man is like deep water, the one who has understanding of this will draw it out." (Proverbs 20:5) NJKV

Using This Book As A Tool

The Journey of Forgiveness is meant to be a devotional guide for inner-healing. It is a 21 day collection of insightful principles that can bring to the reader's conscience and consciousness, personal ownership. *The Journey of Forgiveness* encourages application and responsibility.

I make no claims of having the answers to ultimate healing for anyone. I am sharing from personal practice (experience), principles that work!

The insights are meant for you (the reader) to create a personal list of questions/reflections. Challenge yourself to journal, to consider as authentically as possible how to gain a renewed perspective as it relates to forgiveness. Consideration often opens the heart for Divine counsel.

As you read, take your time. Process only what is needed, discard the rest. Engage yourself – your emotions, thoughts and feelings. Your spirit is highly capable of letting you know what's beneficial, and what's not.

Ask yourself questions, answer if you can, wait for Divine guidance if you can't. As you move throughout your regular schedule of time, learn to trust the intuitive process and the voice of Divine counsel (Holy Spirit). As you trust, you will find that you are moving forward, fully engaged in your journey of forgiveness.

Throughout this collection of insights, *Forgiveness* is a kindred spirit that promotes a lifestyle of accountability and empowerment. I reverence such empowerment within my being, with hopes of you doing the same.

I firmly believe in a Higher Source, in the power of a Holy God Who has equipped us with the authority to change our lives, especially those who rely upon His daily guidance. "It is in Him that we live, move and have our being" ~Acts 17:28

The scriptures declare..."He has given to us all the riches in heavenly places" ~Ephesians 1:3

I consider forgiveness to be one of those riches.

Each of us have enough information stored within us to create life and healing - or death, and destruction. ~Storm

Life Through The Storm: The Journey of Forgiveness
Day 1

Forgiveness ~A Practice of Disciplines

Just as we take daily walks to strengthen our cardiovascular and respiratory systems, to lower the risks of high blood pressure and diabetes; or lift weights to strengthen our muscles - we also need daily disciplines that strengthen and sustain our inner lives. Simply put - disciplines that are beneficial for our overall spiritual, emotional, and psychological well-being must become a part of our daily ritual.

I believe that forgiveness and its maintenance requires some form of discipline. Example – I remember what unforgiveness does to me. It distracts me from what really matters - spiritual, mental and emotional health. So in the event that unforgiveness attempts to entrap me, I do some deep breathing, pray and re-examine my thoughts, expectations, etc. I practice staying on course.

Throughout this book you will encounter many references to prayer, meditation, journaling & deep breathing - my collection of disciplines. You are free to consider my techniques; however, it's important that you practice your preferred discipline. One that centers you for a life of well-being (mind, body & spirit).

What are your daily disciplines (journaling, prayer, deep breathing, etc)?
Do you use it doing stressful times – yes, no – why?
What benefits do you notice...more calm, relaxed or other?
Commit to utilizing your disciplines on a daily basis, this is one of the ways to take ownership of your spirit, your thoughts, and your emotions.

An Excerpt from Life Through The Storm ~The Healing Journey
The practice of forgiveness is a ritual of healthy monitoring of emotional, mental and spiritual influences. It is making sure that debris - via thoughts, daily living, memory, beliefs and perceptions are in alignment with insightful, balanced and conscious living. ~Stormie Steele

Day 2

The Ability To Alter The Moment

We must remind ourselves that the ability to alter our moments is found within our own responses. This is why it's so important to know what we believe, and recognize how those beliefs influence our behavior – our responses.

Forgiveness is the state of being present – attentive and active as life impacts us. I believe that forgiveness equips us with the strength to maintain our healing. Additionally, it supplies us with the insights to discern "what's really important" as we move from scene to scene. Although we may fail the course (the process) from time to time, the discomfort is a quick reminder that we can alter the moment.

Forgiveness then reminds us at moment's notice – that we can, if we are willing - alter any invasion that attempts to hinder our well-being! This is where we pay the closest attention to how we say, whatever it is that we say...when we say it. Especially as it pertains to moments that can feed into unhealthy or bitter encounters. Remember, forgiveness is about self-respect and personal dignity! It gives us ultimate ownership of our emotions.

Forgiveness is not magical...it does not come easily – it is a state of emotional awareness. When we are aware of ourselves (our thinking & our behavior), right then & there we can alter our moments! We can not alter the behavior of others, only our own.

Day 3

Forgiveness ~A Blessing!

Forgiveness is no light matter. It is the blessedness of release from inner-conflict, and a cleansing from unhealthy repetitive replays. A blessing worthy of a life time commitment.

We bring honor to the blessedness of forgiveness each time we remind ourselves to not re-enter the gates of unforgiveness. Examine and re-examine as much as needed if confronted with a conflict (inner or outer), but refute the clutches of unforgiveness!

Forgiveness teaches us to open our eyes, and our ears – giving honor to the many other blessings that daily living offers. Peace of mind, deliverance/release from the impact of a particular offense, and numerous other gifts that are worthy of our attention.

God through His infinite love allows many unexpected life occurrences to nudge us, to assist us in prioritizing our perspective. If we are mindful to view these events as purpose-filled - rather than mere momentary occurrences...we gain much. Look around you, can you give God thanks? If your answer is "Yes", this is another blessing from forgiveness. If "No"...much needs to be considered. You alone can permit forgiveness to take its rightful place.

I remind myself that no matter what the day discloses, there is purpose.
I acknowledge that each moment is significant for my over-all well-being.
God is nudging me into healing - moment by moment!

Day 4

Forgiveness ~A Walk in Mercy, Compassion and Love

We who have walked the path of reclaiming our lives through forgiveness know the challenge of the journey. The journey of forgiveness warrants mercy, compassion and love towards oneself. This knowledge opens a path for us to extend no less than the same towards others. **Note:** This state of being is a significant contribution to our evolution.

When we remember that we too have offended, or have been offensive...there's much room to gain an understanding. Many of us are not alone as we unravel the cords of unforgiveness.

Case and point: Just as it has taken time for me to work through unforgiveness, I extend the same virtues of patience and understanding to those who share in the journey. Especially to those whom I've offended. This does not condone prolonged stay in unhealthy matters, rather – it is a demonstration of
empathy for the human condition. I am a part of the human condition.

As I extend compassion to others, I am refusing judgment or condemnation. I recognize the challenge of forgiveness, as a result - I exude mercy and compassion, love.

An Excerpt from Life Through The Storm ~The Healing Journey
Anyone of us who can attest to living a life of balance and well-being - do so with an allegiance to healthy monitoring...it is a practice. The nuances, idiosyncrasies or minor offenses from others become almost invisible when the practice of forgiveness becomes the norm. ~Stormie Steele

Day 5

Forgiveness and Deep Breathing

I am forever amazed by the power of deep breathing. For me it is one of the simplest ways of coming into a state consciousness and order. Deep breathing is an ancient practice of healing that offers Divine benefits. Research has shown that those who practice deep breathing on a regular basis experience less stress and demonstrate a more centered state of being. Deep breathing exudes healing.

During times of stress, depression or while sulking in thoughts of unforgiveness, we actually hold in the breath with shallow inhalations and exhalations. In other words we constipate and restrict our natural rhythmic flow of healing.

The metaphor of deep breathing is one of drawing in and pushing out, that of opening and closing – receiving and releasing. This constant flow of what to draw in, or what to push out is one of life's continual challenges. Conscious breathing and forgiveness synchronizes our personal rhythm to life.

I understand that there is a time to receive, and a time to let go.
I release the impact of all things (name them) that are not in alignment with Divine order.
I receive all that is good and beneficial for my well-being.

Let's Breathe

Sit in a quiet and comfortable position, clearing your mind from all thoughts and activities of the day. Inhale slowly and naturally through your nose counting to 8, pause for 3 seconds. Exhale slowly and naturally, counting to 11...releasing all thoughts...listening only to the rhythm of your breath. Repeat the above slowly and naturally in a relaxed position for 5 minutes or more, and as many times as possible for complete clearing of emotional debris.

My suggestions are mere considerations - breathe as it feels comfortable and natural for you.

Day 6

Forgiveness ~ Imperfections, Growth & Development

It is one thing to acknowledge one's imperfections, idiosyncrasies and find judgment. It is an entirely different story to acknowledge the same with an intent of growth and development.

Acknowledge that you are in the process of learning how to forgive – first yourself, then others. You will not condemn yourself as you work through this process! This acknowledgment is not a posture of condoning unhealthy thoughts/practices – rather, it is a position of gaining Divine knowledge, understanding, strength, insight and courage. The essential virtues for cleansing and healing.

Forgiveness means that you are facing the aforementioned condition with love, compassion and thoughtfulness. This act of love permeates every fiber of your being...unconditionally.

Learning to forgive myself, teaches me how to forgive others.
I commit to changing those things that disrupt my well-being.

Day 7

Forgiveness ~No Personal Attacks

We can not heal nor forgive ourselves when we attack ourselves through guilt, condemnation or self-pity. It is through acceptance of God's unconditional love for us, and self-acceptance that we begin to heal. We must give ourselves permission to learn through trial & error...no personal attacks. We were not born with the guidelines for living without failure.

When we attack ourselves through guilt and condemnation, we thwart our efforts and pursuits of forgiveness and well-being. Self-acceptance does not declare that we are content with ourselves, it merely means that we embrace our humanity and its need for alignment with a greater Source (God).

Our acceptance of Divine love ushers us to a safe haven that teaches us the meaning of personal love and forgiveness of self, through it all.

Have you ever condemned yourself?
In what ways are you accepting of God's love?
Do you believe that God loves you – Yes, No?
I was not born with the guidelines to live life without failure.

"If we confess our sins, He is faithful and righteous to *forgive* us our sins and to cleanse us from all unrighteousness." ~1 John 1:9

Day 8

Forgiveness and Self-acceptance

When we see ourselves, our authentic selves, it is not to be feared but reverenced. It is then that we can truly begin to uncover the parts of ourselves that have been over looked or under nourished. ~Stormie Steele

I remember as though it were yesterday, I made up in mind to accept all of myself. Armored with determination to overcome, I stood naked in front of a mirror examining my imperfections, inner and outer. I wanted to see all of me (the mirror was a metaphor), the good, the bad and the ugly - all with the intent of acceptance! I was tired of the name calling, the fault finding and all of the blaming for my life's failures.

What I found during that personal inquiry was fear, intelligence, strengths, immaturity, courage, maturity, humor, a sense of hopelessness...and incredible potential! I chose at that moment to commit to honoring the strengths that I had not previously recognized, while working through the weaknesses as best as I could. In other words, I began to care for and to nurture myself!

I knew that my weaknesses needed acceptance (not condoning, but recognition), as all aspects of myself desperately warranted my attention...my guardianship, my love! This arduous process was the genesis of my availability to be accountable for every aspect of my life. No more neglect!

Do you think that you are disregarding yourself in any way?
In what ways have you forgiven yourself?
Unforgiveness towards self is self-defeating...the injured, injuring itself.
I accept my weaknesses as well as my strengths.

Day 9

Forgiveness Virtues

Forgiveness is the meticulous process of patience, love and perseverance. Patience adds virtue to the process of forgiveness, slowly bringing to surface...into view, every facet and particle needed for the journey. Patience teaches us purpose, giving us the invaluable momentum that only participation and time can produce.

Love commands that we authentically respond to the process, meaning that we come out of hiding! No reasons or excuses to justify unforgiveness! We are to be real with ourselves, no matter how difficult the task. This is love's commandment for structuring mind, body, spirit wellness.

Perseverance upholds and structures effort, intent and determination - empowering us with a solid foundation for living.

But let patience have its perfect work, that you may be perfect and complete, lacking nothing.
~~James 1:4 (NKJV)

I allow patience to produce within me value and sacred regard for my life.
I lovingly participate in my healing.
As I endure, I am strengthened with the courage to continue.

Day 10

Forgiveness ~Seize The Evolution!

Forgiveness is work! It is more than, "I forgive you"...it is an emotional,, spiritual and life-altering evolution! When we forgive, we seize every moment of doingmthe thing that we know to do - taking full opportunity of time.

Time offers the injured soul opportunities to heal through every day occurrences – we literally seize our evolution as we participate. In part this means living with our eyes wide open.

When we consciously engage daily living, we seize our evolution through the many moments that beckon our attention! Activating whatsoever our personal evolution is requiring of us.

Each day I open myself to learn.

I trust that God is working on my behalf for good.

I am alert and actively seizing each moment.

Day 11

Forgiveness and The Offender

Forgiveness means that you have taken the offender and all of the offenses of such, out of your thought life - away from your emotional well-being and far removed from your present state of being!

Forgiveness means that we have ultimate control and ownership of how we are impacted by life's unfortunate encounters. We must be on guard (not paranoid) regarding how we resolve painful matters. In the long run, forgiveness serves the forgiver's highest good. The offender is often absent from the dilemmas of the offended.

Forgiveness can be challenging, yet-if we can remember how liberated we were from previous experiences, perhaps forgiveness can be more readily pursued. Unforgiveness and self-destruction are in the same category - self-defeating!

We're not hurting the offender when we choose unforgiveness, we hurt ourselves. Learn to forgive - it makes healthy sense - your mind, your body and your spirit will gain the benefit.

An Excerpt from Life Through The Storm ~The Healing Journey

The past with all of its influences (especially negative impacts)...its beliefs and patterns have passed. Healing is knowing this truth, while living far removed from its impact. Living beyond the past continues to be an intentional practice of chosen principles & techniques (prayer, forgiveness, wisdom, meditation, journaling, affirmations or other...) that create a new way of observing and processing life's encounters. ~Storm

The Alteration of Forgiveness

Forgiveness alters us emotionally, psychologically and spiritually. It is an alteration of our beliefs, our speech, and our behavior. Those words that we once spoke to ourselves through shame, guilt or lack of self-love are no longer allowed entry. Additionally, words that we once spoke regarding others through anger, hurt, resentment, or lacking in love are no longer allowed.

We have exchanged self-defeating habits, and their dynamics through the power of Divine knowledge, understanding and wisdom. The utilization of this power alters us, assisting us forward - step by step as we dissolve out-dated familiar behavior.

Those things that I once spoke, I will no longer allow.
I am released from anything that creates inner-dis-ease!
I am making full use of the knowledge of God within my life!
I speak new life to my soul...today!!

"Forgiveness is me giving up my right to hurt you for hurting me."
- Anonymous

Day 13

Forgiveness ~Know That You Are Loved

So many of us have sought for love outside of ourselves for so long that we've forgotten that the greatest impact of her awareness comes from God...within. God is love! When we accept love...everything changes, our thoughts, our beliefs, our behavior and our sense of worth.

Knowing that we are loved is life altering! But how can we know love...if we've not experienced it from within ourselves?

No one has ever been, nor will they ever be responsible to love us greater than the love that is given to us from God...and from ourselves.

Knowing that I am loved keeps me open to possibility. Forgive yourself and recognize that you are loved.

God is the only One Who can accept me unconditionally.
I work to give to myself that same degree of unconditional love.
I am loved, I have always been loved...I will always be loved!

Day 14

Forgiveness ~Not an Easy Task

As easy as it sounds forgiveness can be one of the most challenging paths to take. Maybe we think that it has something to do with the offender getting away with a particular offense – they're not getting what we think they deserve. Ultimately, forgiveness is not about the offender, it's about you. Forgiveness in no wise condones offenses – it liberates us from further injury.

I say it often as a word of encouragement – forgiveness is about self-preservation - a way of preserving our sanity and dignity. Forgiveness gives us the rightful place-ownership of our emotions and overall well-being.

We too offend...whether we admit it or not. Others are perhaps attempting to be liberated from something that we said or did to them. When you recognize or suspect that you've offended someone, don't hesitate to ask them for forgiveness – pride destroys much more than our relationships!

"When you hold resentment toward another, you are bound to that person or condition by an emotional link that is stronger than steel. Forgiveness is the only way to dissolve that link and get free." ~Katherine Ponder

Day 15

Forgiveness ~The Command of Quiet

It is quite possible to quieten the self, to discipline and control inner noise. When we give ourselves permission to enter such a place, we create for ourselves a sense of relief through any circumstance that seems to be overwhelming.

We command the quiet – consciously and intentionally. As we learn to empty ourselves of unforgiveness, we open powerful doors for healing...the command of quiet is one of them!

Stop, pay close attention to where you are at this very moment.

Engage the moment, the calm – the quiet.

As I forgive those who have offended me, it's needful to remember - I too have offended.

Day 16

Forgiveness ~Waking Up from A Bad Dream,

Unforgiveness is at the helm of personal and relational instability. Unforgiveness hinders our perspective of possibility, within ourselves as well as in others.

Unforgiveness separates us from inner healing and ultimately from ourselves. Unforgiveness is at the core of inner-dis-ease (discord, resentment, etc). Whenever we refuse to forgive, we spread its venom to those around us.

Unforgiveness blocks the possibility of a full recovery! Unforgiveness is a set-back, one that delays inner growth and emotional stability.

I am the first to admit that forgiveness is not always a simple task, nevertheless - it's pursuit is worthy of engaging. Believe me, those who dare embrace forgiveness will gain far more than they imagined. Below is my list of reminders. I hope that you too will find them useful.

Forgiveness is like waking up from a bad dream, and realizing that you've missed all the important dates & numerous years of living. I too have faced the brutal effects of unforgiveness.

Forgiveness is a journey of self-love, one that grants personal ownership and empowerment. Forgiveness is the virtue that comes closest to touching the heart of God.

Forgiveness is a matter of self-preservation - a matter of personal development and a matter of spiritual awareness. Forgiveness is the soul's deep cleanser.

Forgiveness gives us the ability to triumph over unexplainable offenses – permitting us to live!

Forgiveness is not about "them" or what "they" did...it's about me!

Day 17

Imagine Forgiveness

Can you imagine for one moment what it would be like to forgive those who **have offended** you...or those whom you **believe have offended** you? How do you think that you would feel? What type of thoughts could you replace with unforgiveness?

As I recognize my own hurts, it becomes easier to recognize the feelings of those whom I've hurt. I remind myself that others really are no different than I am, especially if they have been hurt or misunderstood. As I replay an experience of having been offended, others tend to do no less of the same. I empathize and imagine forgiveness becoming a reality.

It's disturbing and disappointing to know that I can cause pain to someone - yet, it's a reality. With this awareness, I pay closer attention to how I interact with others. Holding myself responsible and accountable for what I say is paramount!

Whether an offense is intentional (spoken in anger), or unintentional...it needs to be acknowledged. An apology is one of the basic ways in which we show respect & regard towards one another. Furthermore, we give to ourselves and to those whom we have offended a chance to move more rapidly from dis-ease.

When I imagine forgiveness, it seems simple. In reality, it's more than a notion - it is a labor of love – humility and conscious effort!

"We are all on a life long journey and the core of its meaning, the terrible demand of its centrality is forgiving and being forgiven."
~Martha Kilpatrick

Day 18

Resentment, an Inner Alarm

When it comes to my inner life, I pay attention to my internal alarm-it alerts me when things are out of order. For example – I remember the very moment that I had a sense of resentment towards another person. I won't go into the details, rather, I will elaborate on the feelings that were evoked during that emotion.

Simply stated, I felt an endless need for an apology! No matter how many apologies were given, I still felt that "**it wasn't enough**!". So, I asked myself a question, "**Am I resentful**?". The need to ask such a question was based on an apparent "**hardness of my heart**" - it was stuck! After an affirmative "Yes!", an immediate sense of shame and remorse took over. I acknowledged that it was in fact resentment! The awareness of such prompted a need to forgive the offender, and deal with myself!

That being said, I've experienced the need to forgive plenty of times; yet, I had not allowed those times prolonged stay, festering into resentment. Were the previous injuries (perceived or other) not deep enough to warrant resentment? Whatever the reason - to date, there has not been a reason, or an excuse worthy of harboring emotions leading to resentment!!

Resentment is resulted from long-term unforgiveness, it is relentless. Those feelings metastasize (for the lack of a better word), turning into harsher feelings. Additionally, resentment can take root when offenses are repetitious in nature, with no apologies or an acknowledgment of wrong from the offender. How long does it take for resentment to set in? I don't know. Our personal experiences vary.

My experience in resentment was a result of having not faced, nor dealt with an unhealthy situation in the first place! Had I been responsible & taken the necessary steps to get out "sooner than later", no doubt – resentment would have been avoided. I held myself hostage in resentment long enough to learn a powerful lesson – it was possible to turn into someone that I did not want to be!

"Resentment is often a woman's inner signal that she has been ignoring an important God-given responsibility - that of making choices." ~Brenda Waggoner

"God is always trying to give blessings to us, but our minds are usually too full to receive them." ~Shannon L. Alder

"As smoking is to the lungs, so is resentment to the soul; even one puff is bad for you." ~Elizabeth Gilbert

Day 19

Lessons in Forgiveness

I've learned a lot about forgiveness. So when I encourage others to consider engaging in the same, I do so with a full understanding...it is not as easy as it sounds. I stress forgiveness so often because without it, many other aspects of healthy living can be hindered .

Unforgiveness is contagious. When we speak our ill feelings to people who are themselves embattled with unforgiveness – it potentially creates an even more dark and gloomy perspective, an almost hopeless state of existence. Can you imagine the energy flow of people who are constantly talking through the dark glasses of unforgiveness? Resentful and bitter words (repetitively spoken) are unnecessary, ugly, and detrimental!

One of my most prolific truths-finding the strength and courage to forgive in one area of my life... trickling into other needed areas.

I've forgiven those who exposed me to childhood abuse. I have forgiven those who took advantage of the innocent me. I've forgiven myself for the times that I was foolish – not wise in weighing the pros and cons of particular situations. As foolish as it sounds, I've even forgiven God - Whom I thought was at fault at times too! The list goes on and on...

Across the board forgiveness means that I don't have the room in my life to linger in unforgiveness - period! Prolonged unforgiveness distorts/detracts the truth of who we are. Across the board forgiveness is healthy – mind, body, spirit!

Day 20

Forgiveness ~Seventy Times Seventy

I know from personal experience that forgiveness works, it is life-altering! Jesus reminds us to forgive seventy times seventy (Matthew 18:21-22). That's a lot of forgiving! It's one of the most challenging paths to take. Perhaps we think that our offender is getting away with a particular offense, maybe we think that they deserve far more than being forgiven. The truth of the matter is this - forgiveness is not about the offender, it's about you. Forgiveness in no wise condones offenses – it liberates its victims from further injury.

I've watched myself over the years mentally experience and re-experience a particular painful memory – only to set myself up for an emotional set-back! I'd end up attacking myself with self-injurious words because of someone else's offense.

Unforgiveness is relentless – it's psychologically destructive. I can remember speaking to a previous offender about the pain caused by their behavior – the person had no recollection of what I was talking about! A huge wake-up call for me! I couldn't believe that I had to walk through the doors of forgiving them without a simple act of human courtesy - an apology.

"Resentment is like drinking poison and then hoping it will kill your enemies." ~Nelson Mandela

Forgiveness is about self-preservation - a way of preserving our sanity and dignity. Forgiveness further gives us the rightful place of ownership of our emotions and overall well-being. Forgive – it's not easy...it's a process of time. Your mind, body and spirit will gain a life worthy of its benefits.

Day 21

Forgiveness ~Reconciliation

Forgiveness does not always mean relational reconciliation – although at times, it does. Forgiveness is reconciling within oneself, the issue that will not be reconciled with another. Additionally – forgiveness is an emotional cleansing – an offering of healing, a renewal of perspective.

Forgiveness is an act of will, that of reconciling issues…and the impact of such within oneself. Forgiveness is a worthy investment (mind, body, spirit). Make the most of your time and your life…reconcile and forgive.

Unforgiveness is inner dis-ease - an enemy of love-leading its followers into cycles of spiritual/personal neglect, victimization and blame.
~Stormie G. Steele

A Brief Prayer for Your Journey of Forgiveness

I appreciate your purchase of this book, but mostly - your desire to forgive. As you commit to the process of time, and all that it warrants, you'll find that you've made a worthy investment. I pray that you will find the strength within that guides you forward in every way possible. With God all things are possible!

Your commitment and faithfulness towards God – yourself and your beliefs will ultimately lead you to experience healing (mind, body, spirit). May you find balance, and the needed perspective that aids in your journey to forgive. The God of all peace equip you with every heavenly blessing designed to bring an inner-evolution, surpassing all disappointments!

"Now unto him that is able to do exceeding abundantly above all that we ask or think, according to the power that worketh in us..." ~Ephesians 3:20 (KJV)

About The Author

Stormie G. Steele is the founder of Life Through The Storm, a ministry encouraging spiritual & personal development into more than 100 countries around the world. She holds a doctorate in holistic life counseling, recognizing The Holy Spirit as The Supreme Voice of counsel.

Stormie has over 20 years experience as a broadcaster - lending her talents in both television and radio. Her voice has graced the airways-serving Christian, gospel, urban contemporary, smooth jazz and traditional jazz formats.

Steele's love for the African drum (djembe) has blended with musical genres including: contemporary Christian, inspirational, country, new age, African rhythms and adult contemporary.

She enjoys teaching on spiritual and personal development.

Other books from the author:

Life Through The Storm ~The Healing Journey (available in ebook and print)

Life Through The Storm ~Healthy Relationships (available in ebook and print)

Connect with Me On-line

Life Through The Storm:

Website: http://www.stormiesteele.com/
Twitter: htttp://www.twitter.com/stormiegsteele
Instagram: http://www.instagram.com/stormiesteele

Bible quotations in this volume are from King James Version, New American Standard, New International Version, and New Standard Version

Forgiveness Quotes –

Nelson Mandela Goodreads.com
Katherine Ponder & Martha Kilpatrick @ www.psychologytoday.com

Thomas Merton, Brenda Waggoner, Shannon L. Alder, and Elizabeth Gilbert @ www.goodreads.com

www.ingramcontent.com/pod-product-compliance
Lightning Source LLC
Chambersburg PA
CBHW062055090426
42740CB00016B/3147